CW00556570

Foot Reading

A simple guide
which explains the principles and
applications of Foot Reading and it's
good fun as well

Foot Reading

Published by
Douglas Barry Publications

Tel : 020 8680 9631
E-mail dbarrypubs@aol.com

Foot Reading
FIRST EDITION 2001

COPYRIGHT 2001
©RENÉE TANNER

All Rights Reserved. No part of this publication may be reproduced or transmitted in any form or by any means, electronic or mechanical, including photocopying, recording, or any information storage or retrieval system, without prior written permission of the author, Renée Tanner. Nor may it be otherwise circulated in any form of binding or cover other than that in which it is published and without similar condition being imposed on the subsequent purchaser. Written in 2001

British Library - A CIP Catalogue record for this book is available from the British Library.

I.S.B.N.   0-9516203-7-1

Acknowledgements

I acknowledge the support of my long suffering family during the year of preparation of this book.

I would like to single out for mention Russell to whom I am most appreciative for his patience and support whilst this book developed from my pen into the finished manuscript. I am indebted to Adriana Brinsmead-Stockham and Carole & Sid Leftwich for their generous input of time and support.

I should mention here also all my past and current students for their encouragement and without whom this book might not have materialised.

My thanks to Ed Morrison for his drawings and to David English for the cover image.

About the Author

Renée began studying feet during the early sixties while working as a pedicurist. Fascinated by the differences, not only in comparison to the opposite foot but relative to the foot being examined, she went on to explore her theories over a period of some thirty years and thousands of pairs of feet.

This book is the result of a compilation of notes and observations and began its life as a book following numerous teaching sessions and requests for further information.

Your Feet

In the average 70 year lifetime our feet cover 70,000 miles, which is approximately 1,000 miles per year.

In that 70 year lifetime we walk an equivalent distance of 2° times around the world.

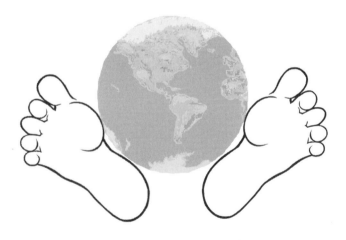

Note To The Reader
Disclaimer

Neither the author nor publisher can accept any responsibility whatsoever for any health problem which results from the use of the methods described in this book.

This book is not intended as a substitute for professional or medical advice.

The reader is urged to consult a general medical practitioner as to the cause or nature of a health problem of any sort.

Introduction

Foot reading developed as a natural progression from dealing with feet over a period of more than thirty five years.

As a young therapist I was fascinated by toe shapes and sizes, I recall making notes about changes and/or abnormalities being related to a specific characteristic.

As time passed my interest developed from toes to the whole foot, I have written this book as a way of sharing my knowledge with a far wider audience.

I have chosen the format for ease and yet to encourage you the reader to use your own judgement in bringing together a conclusion.

When you first begin to read feet, take care with your outspoken language. Be sensitive and aware of other people's feelings.

It is not the intention of this book to give a complete character analysis of the user/reader. To achieve such magnitudes this book would need to include a reading on every minute line and mark appropriate to every fraction of an inch relative to each foot.

The interpretations could then need years of experience to perfect.

What I have given the reader is a taster and hopefully awakened an interest in the fascinating subject of foot reading.

Author's Notes

While I refer to reflex areas throughout this book, it is in no way intended to be a Reflexology Book.
However, qualified Reflexologists may use the application form within these pages to request information relative to Reflexology.

I have always encouraged people to learn as much about themselves as possible. One good way to begin this is to learn about their own feet. Many people only look at their own feet when they are washing or creaming them, cutting their nails or applying nail polish.

Does the foot reader need to be psychic or intuitive? No, foot reading relies on neither quality, it is all written in the feet for anyone to read. However those with psychic and/or intuitive qualities may well use these qualities to support their foot reading skills.

While this introduction is a comprehensive piece of work, there is room for expansion and I am currently looking at the possibility of a follow up book.

How to use this book

This book is written in the main assuming one foot or the other is dominant, however should both feet present demonstrating similar characteristics then read both columns. Be aware one foot or toe will usually be more dominant than the other. Before coming to any conclusion, ensure that you examine the right and left foot carefully, as the differences may be very subtle.

With practice and experience you will become very efficient in your task and be able to recognise changes almost immediately you glance at the feet.

THE ANGLE OF THE FOOT

Examining The Foot Angle

When examining angles of the foot / feet, we look first at the foot from the natural standing position, or better still, look at the two feet when the owner is lying on a couch or bed. When examining your own feet look at the stance looking down onto the feet and while you are lying on the floor or on a bed or couch and look at the soles in a mirror. In this relaxed state the feet tend to fall into a natural position.

A fun thing to do while practising your new found skill is to observe the angles of the feet of your households and / or guests. This method of observation could also be practised on colleagues at work or people standing in a supermarket queue. You will soon come to realise that very few people hold both feet pointing straight, and you will begin to ask "why?"

LEFT FOOT

LEFT FOOT TURNED IN
RIGHT FOOT NORMAL UPRIGHT POSITION

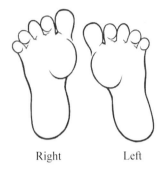

Right   Left

Dealing with changes in life
May be dealing with current emotional difficulties
Has overcome some unhappiness from the past
Great understanding for others and their feelings
Will be there if needed, just ask
A strong shoulder for others to cry on

LEFT FOOT TURNED OUT
RIGHT FOOT NORMAL UPRIGHT POSITION

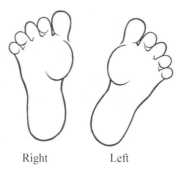

Right   Left

May have difficulty to express emotions
Possibly a past hurt is safely tucked away
May get by in life without bearing his/her soul
May currently be involved in or has left a less than
satisfactory relationship
What others think does matter to the owner of these feet

RIGHT FOOT

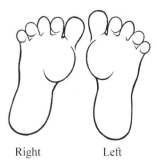

Right   Left

Issues of the past influence everyday life
May go through long periods of uncertainty
Always searching for answers
May suffer occasional bouts of depression
Forging ahead towards progress, trying to leave the past
behind
Tries to please everyone

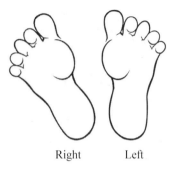

Right   Left

The past has a huge influence on the present
May have difficulty letting go of past issues
Feels there are some things best not said
May feel that they have made a wrong decision in
the past but can live with it
Usually a very good listener

BOTH FEET

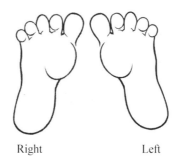

Right   Left

Possibly shy

May be self-conscious, but none-the-less capable

Feels insecure but can do the work and does not like to be observed

May show extreme nervousness when put under pressure leading to failure or lower grade in examinations

May not be good at interview techniques

Usually there to offer help to anyone in need

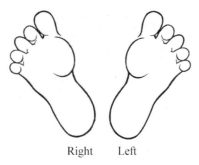

Right   Left

May be off track
Not necessarily own decider
May seem to follow in someone else's footsteps
May feel dominated in the home or work place
Constantly following instructions, may be
an actor, actress or forces personnel
Accommodating person

FOOT TYPES

EXAMINING FOOT TYPES

When examining foot types, the size of the foot is relative to body size.

Example / guide

1. A 6ft (1.83m) - 14 stone (90.7kg) male with size 7 (41) shoes would be considered as having small feet.

2. A 5ft 3" (1.60m) - 8st 2lb (51.7kg) female wearing size 6 (39) shoes would be considered to have large feet

Foot Types

Firm and Inflexible   -   Orderly work pattern
May be set in their ways
May not like to give way but
often will

Firm and Flexible   -   Orderly manner
Copes well
Not very impressionable
May feel a constant need to
improve

Flaccid and Soft   -   Soft nature
Gives in to others needs/demands
Capable of great things but does
not necessarily achieve desired
heights
Supports others

Soft and Inflexible   -   Soft nature
Huge barriers of defence

Hard course skin   -   True thoughts / feelings hidden
Protecting vulnerability
A barrier to hide behind
May have a tendency to be
stubborn

Broad Feet	-	Spends life enjoying doing for others
Both feet large	-	May feel they fight for survival Practical talents tend to be more obvious
Both feet small	-	May feel that there are some external restraints May feel life has not allowed room for true emotional expansion
Wrinkled Feet	-	Anxious Thoughtful of the needs of others before self
Swollen / swellings	-	May feel weighed down with life Unresolved emotions Hidden tears
Flattened Areas	-	Drained energy Resistance to going forward may detour but gets there in the end Due to a fear of failing, may have initial hesitancy to try something new

FOOT STANCE

Flat Foot   -   May feel weighed down with life's problems
Perceived pressure from family, work or friends
Usually kind and thoughtful
May need support
May be overworked
Possibly overweight

FOOT STANCE
WALKING OR STANDING

Tiptoe   -   Does not wish to attract attention
May suffer a slight to major inferiority complex
Feels more capable than is recognised by others
May have an inquisitive mind, wants to see and hear more

DIFFERENCES IN THE SHAPE AND SIZE OF FEET

DIFFERENCES IN SHAPE AND SIZE OF THE FEET
RIGHT VERSUS LEFT FOOT

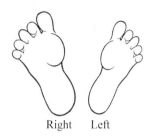

Right   Left

RIGHT FOOT

Larger	-	Possibly felt a little less restricted in earlier life than in the present
Smaller	-	Possibly felt a little more restricted in earlier life than in the present
Heavier	-	Emotions of the earlier life may still be inflicting burden
Misshapen	-	Some character changes may be due to past experiences and pressures
Tense	-	Possible past conflict with a male Possible present or past work related conflict with more than one male

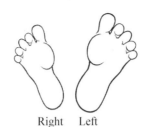

Right   Left

LEFT FOOT

Larger   -   May have learned to hide inhibitions
                            Possibly a degree more freedom in the
                            present than in the past

Smaller   -   Presently may feel more confined and
                            restrained mentally and/or physically
                            than in the past

Heavier   -   May be leading a more demanding
                            lifestyle now than in the past
                            May feel expected to shoulder more
                            responsibility than in the past

Misshapen   -   Difficulties standing up for self
                            Being unfairly pressured
                            May be taking care of others

Tense   -   Possible past dispute with a female
                            Possible present or past work related
                            conflict with more than one female

TOP OF THE FOOT

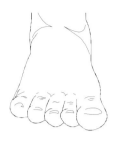

Bunion raised on
top of foot   -   Can be inflexible
                                        Feels committed to others
                                        Would like to change life style

Bunion on
side of foot   -   Others come before self
                                        May feel restrained
                                        Possible strict upbringing
                                        Possibly had some sorrow in life
                                        especially if big toe is displaced

Burning feeling   -   May feel everyone is not treating
                                        them fairly
                                        May have suffered some injustices in
                                        life resulting in stuck energy
                                        May be focusing on a problem

Large dark marks   -   May feel let down by a close friend or
                                        family member

Fat pads   -   Building a resistance to pressure
                                        Hides feelings
                                        Protection from the demands
                                        of others

 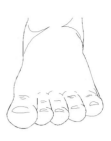

Hairy — Protection from being very
sensitive

Itching — May be a little impatient
Not always tolerant
Wants to express ideas

Ligaments obvious — May feel held back
May feel unable to move forward at
desired pace
Needs support for own ideas

Protruding bones — Feels he/she is expected to or has in
the past been expected to meet
dead lines and demands of others

Red — May feel back is against the wall
May feel all their energy is being
drained away

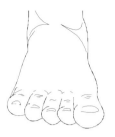 

Sunken   -   May feel they have done all possible
                         to help others
                         May have used most of their energy
                         reserves trying to acheive their aims

Swollen   -   Possible unshed tears
                         Life may have influenced a heavy
                         burden

Wrinkled   -   May be tired of all that is going on
                         around them
                         Fighting to meet all the demands
                         on his/her time

SOLE OF THE FOOT

Foot - Sole

Peeling foot	-	A sign of change Possible progression May finally be ready to accept or understand a situation A worrier A fear of change and failure
Sweaty feet	-	Emotional or physical overload May feel unappreciated Not often praised as deserved May have felt put down as a child
Bumps (red)	-	Built up emotions Home life not as first appears Anger and disappointment (the degree depends on the spread of the bumps)
Bumps (white)	-	Work life may not be as first appears May have some difficulty being self-expressive in the workplace Would like more choice Dominent parent / guardian / teacher

Full Fat Mound (in ball of foot)-   May have energy in peaks, very low
to very high
Really does get choked up at times
May have taken on a lot in life

Very, Very Lined (going in all directions)-
 Overworked
 Plenty of stress
 A most capable person
 Capabilities may not always be obvious

Callous around edge   -   Digging the heels in
Protection
Subconscious fear of pregnancy
Subconscious fear of commitment
Reinforces defences
Extra protection and defences to
stand up for self
May be a little stubborn

Bone growth at back of heel   -   Feeling held back
Constantly trying to overcome
obstacles
Enters competitions as a sports
person but is not always mentally
prepared

Dark dots/marks   -   Experienced real or perceived
prejudices, possibly gender, age,
education, colour or religious
Deep hurt due to emotional restriction
Not recognised for capabilities and
achievements

Cracked	-	Pulled in different directions Does not know which way to turn Changes taking place cause inner turmoil Feels a need to please everyone
Shiny	-	Faced resistance from others to ideas for most of life Really tries not to cause friction Possibly bullied in a very manipulative way
Bruised	-	Movements blocked A desire to move on A fear of a perceived hurtful recent situation A fear of a perceived hurtful situation ahead
Swollen	-	Bogged down A lack of energy No enthusiasm to make changes A perceived block to future success

Wrinkled — Stuck in a rut
Concerned about the future
Feels insecure
Would love to be able to turn the clock back

Burning feeling — Current lifestyle infuriates
Work situation creates a burning desire for change
Consumed with ambition to create
A burning desire to achieve and move forward

Cold — Lacks enthusiasm for change
Not very confident especially in relation to change
A capable person but fears failure
When the pressure is on gets cold feet especially at the last minute

THE ANKLE

INNER ANKLE

Sunken   -   Possible emotional overload
                                          May have had a shock

Swollen / Prominent   -   Resentment at the injustices of life
                                          Draws strength from within
                                          Undealt with emotions

Broken veins / Colour change-   Suppressed emotions emerging
                                          Inner turmoil being dealt with
                                          Greater understanding and acceptance
                                          of what life has issued

OUTER ANKLE

Fat Pads   -   May be feeling insecure
                        Building barriers to protect emotions
                        Life may be all work and little play

Swollen   -   Believes material possessions can be
                        a substitute for emotional loss
                        May be a hoarder (squirrel like)
                        Does not always pay attention to
                        health warnings
                        May fear promotion or extra
                        responsibility

Red   -   Possibly some pent up anger at
                        perceived lack of support in either
                        home or work

TOES

 # TOE READING

When reading this section, comparisons and changes should be examined in the context of the foot / feet being read.

Out of proportion infers comparison with other toes, this can vary from a slight change to a total difference, some changes will be very evident and some will need close examination in order to be noticeable.

A long toe, one that is longer than either of its neighbours or equal in length to one or both neighbours. In the case of the big toe, this will be seen to be much longer than might be expected of a big toe.

A broad base is relative to the toe being examined.

A narrow middle joint is relative to the toe being examined.

A broad top joint is relative to the toe being examined.

A thin toe in comparison to other toes.

A broad toe in comparison to other toes.

The explanations set out in the columns will be read bearing in mind the degrees of change - from definite to a tendency towards to a possible tendency towards

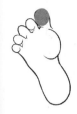

Big Toe
Broad base / Neck of toe

RIGHT	LEFT
Reliable	Helpfull
Modest	Emotional argument may take priority over rational argument
Busy doing more than one thing at a time	Would never want to cheat on a partner
Possibly in the service of others	Needs to guard against being too much of the same all the time
Usually knows what they want, but does not always have the courage to go and get it	Does not always let others know how they are feeling about certain situations
	Kind person

Big Toe
Narrow base / Neck of toe

RIGHT	LEFT
Keeps thoughts close to chest	Hidden strength
Determined spirit	When pushed will be able to stand up for self
Will test the waters before announcing new ideas	Full of surprises
Some very good ideas, but not necessarily in a position to develop them	Probably once felt cramped and dominated/bullied by tutor/trainer/ older school boy or girl
	Wary of expressing emotions
	What others think and say will probably affect the owner of these feet

Big Toe
Broad from the neck to the Tip of Toe

Right

Left

Has learned to stand on own two feet quite well

May fantasise and day dream

Enthusiastic but might be limited to one main area of interest

Dislikes confrontation/ arguments but will usually stand up for own rights, possibly more so in the family setting

Needs to guard against allowing enthusiasm to unnecessarily expand the story

Likes a peaceful life

Can lose confidence in own abilities

Emotional loss may have long term effect

Needs to bounce ideas off friends, but does not necessarily want opinions

May possibly be manipulated by a partner or friend but would not believe or accept that this is so

Does not suffer fools gladly

Loyal friend

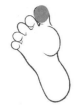 

BIG TOE
LONG

RIGHT	**LEFT**
Achiever	Lots of energy
May have lots to say for themselves	Capable of great clarity of thought
Academic strengths	May suffer depression due to perceived need to be the best at all that is attempted
Confident	Considerate
Independent	
May sometimes have head in the clouds	
May display completely opposite tendencies to what might be expected	

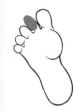

SECOND TOE
LONGER THAN BIG TOE

RIGHT	LEFT
Potential for great leadership	Only one soul mate in life
Moves quickly with promotion in job	Capable of making all relationships special
Clear analytical mind	Makes others feel good about themselves
May have psychic abilities	Magnet for opposite sex
Healing powers	Capable of deep love
Integrates with ease	Capable of hiding true feelings
Capable of standing alone	May carry scars of past loves
Instills confidence in others	May suffer or have already suffered a letdown or perceived letdown by partner
Clear thinker	

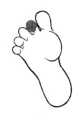

SECOND TOE
SLIGHTLY OUT OF PROPORTION IN
COMPARISON TO OTHER TOES

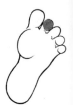

RIGHT	LEFT
Clear thinker	Attracts others
Success with potential for more	Capable of deep love but of hiding true feelings
Integrates with ease	May carry scars of past hurt
Enjoys own company	May suffer as a result of perceived letdown in a close relationship

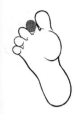

SECOND TOE
VERY BROAD / OUT OF PROPORTION IN COMPARISON TO OTHER TOES

RIGHT	LEFT
May feel life's burden is heavier than it could or should be	May feel weighed down with emotional turmoil
Might not make friends easily but will usually keep friends	May have experienced, or be experiencing some sadness
Feels everything in life has to be worked for	May have a tendency to suffer with depression or mood swings
May not be enjoying current lifestyle/work	May turn to excesses in social habits, sport, exercise or work
Might have a tendency to be stubborn	
Will probably know lots of people, but consider few in the special position of friend	

SECOND TOE
SLIGHTLY BROAD / OUT OF PROPORTION IN
COMPARISON TO OTHER TOES

RIGHT	LEFT
Good listener	Don't try to fool this person
Analyses every word though may not give that impression	Intends to make absolute right choice when choosing a partner or won't bother with permenancy
Diligent worker or quite lazy	Why can't people understand what is said is what is meant
Others need to prove abilities before being trusted	Usually not first child in family or may have a close relationship with young mother or aunt
Might have slight dogmatic tendencies	Will listen, may or may not act
Friendship is always respected	A good confidant

70

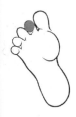 

SECOND TOE
BROAD BASE

RIGHT	LEFT
Strong mind	Perhaps security or attachment to one person was longed for in young life
Inner desire to achieve a lot in life	Perceived let down in childhood or early adulthood
May want more than childhood offered	Perhaps only child or after a number of years another child or person joined the family
Life may now be more structured than in early childhood	A willing helper
A solid friend	

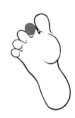 

SECOND TOE
BROAD TOP JOINT

RIGHT	LEFT
May be experiencing a lifestyle change	Attitude is probably, I won't be hurt and would not let people know if I was
Probably achieves a lot in life	Life probably dished out a bad deal, but attitude is probably so what if it did
I'll be the person I am	A willing helper, dependable friend
I have probably overcome my past uncertainties	May go over the top to protect emotions
Recovered from a mild illness or accident	

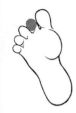

SECOND TOE
NARROW MIDDLE JOINT

RIGHT	LEFT
Perhaps trying too hard to overcome a perceived failure	The sensitive nature of this person may lead them to believe they are / were dominated by trainer /tutor / nanny or carer
May have some difficulties expressing true potential	Life's love and desires not fully achieved
Perceived own character / views and needs just choked out	A possible lost love
May sometimes feel anger / frustration	May believe they could not meet expectations of others
Lots of brain power, but it is not always used to its full capacity	A caring nature

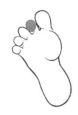

SECOND TOE
VERY THIN

RIGHT | **LEFT**

Feels able to stand alone

Strong Hidden emotions

Can deal with more than one problem at a time

Attracts others not necessarily always suitable

May be a good negotiator

May have been let down by a partner or worry that this could happen

Will usually do what they set out to do

May see own relationship with partner as unusual

Ability to smooth things over

Sensitive nature / cares what others think

Hard worker

May feel unable to work in a particular place or to socialise due to perceived gossiping of others

SECOND TOE
TILTING TOWARDS TOE ONE

RIGHT	LEFT
May have learned a lesson in life	May lack confidence in feelings / emotions
Doubts about expressing own ideas	May suppress feelings
Believes life might have dealt short change	May be afraid to try again (protection of self)
Tries to focus on one thing	May be thinking more deeply or studying more than in the past
Tries to get it right	May have returned to learning
Probably reads a lot and / or is involved in producing / designing something	Thinking of taking on something involved in caring profession, or perhaps voluntary?

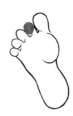

SECOND TOE
TILTS TOWARDS TOE THREE

RIGHT

LEFT

Possibly a change taking place

Creativity helps with
emotional expression

Trying to be more direct in expression

May look back on love /
relationships

Some aspects of life may have been
better in the past

Something to show for life :-
gardening - sewing - carpentry
- complementary therapy, etc.

May work in a caring
profession or feel responsible
for a family member

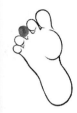

THIRD TOE
VERY BROAD / OUT OF PROPORTION

RIGHT

LEFT

Very hard worker

Hidden potential creativity

Workaholic tendencies

Ability to reach great height in chosen creativity

Tackle any task

Needs to guard against impatience to detail

Will just keep going

Thinks a lot before starting something new

Heavy engine type slog - slog

THIRD TOE
SLIGHTLY BROAD / OUT OF PROPORTION TO OTHERS

RIGHT	LEFT
Hard worker	Likes it to look just right but always better if someone else makes it so
Acts and listens at the same time	Has good potential for creativity but does not always put it to use
Reliable	May have a few projects in the pipeline at any one time
Won't be pushed too far	

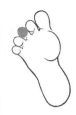

THIRD TOE
BROAD BASE

RIGHT	LEFT
Possible change of direction in early life	Influenced by emotions
Puts effort into getting what they want	May be influenced by intellectuals
Always wanted to achieve	Watch for quick temper although short lived
May have sought attention all through life and yet did not always get recognition	Inventive mind
Possibly a determined type	Good imagination but this may be deeply hidden

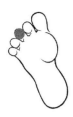

THIRD TOE
BROAD TOP JOINT

RIGHT	LEFT
Finally I have shown them I can do it	There may be a change of cultural habits
I will carry on standing up for my own rights and those of others	Creative flair/talents
May seem aggressive when what is intended is positive action	Finally found an outlet for talents
A solid type	Reliable friend
	May really care what others think, and be affected by that

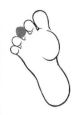

THIRD TOE
NARROW MIDDLE JOINT

RIGHT

LEFT

Some ideas squashed by others

Creativity dampened

May not have been able to take up employment / education at time of life that would be most appropriate

Outside influences may cramp or be perceived to do so

May have to try hard to assert rights

May now think original ideas on creativity were way out?

Does not feel a free spirit

Something may have prevented this creative mind developing along the normal lines

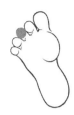

THIRD TOE
LONG (MAY BE EQUAL TO TOE TWO)

RIGHT

LEFT

Thinks and acts at the same time

Creativity feeds on emotion

Decisive

Difficulty in separating creativity and emotions

Enthusiastic

Inventive

Strong survival instinct

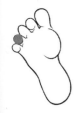

FOURTH TOE
BROAD / OUT OF PROPORTION

RIGHT | **LEFT**

Hoards anything and everything

Hard worker

A solid friend

Enjoys permanency

Possibly restricted in early life from following a passion - music, drama, painting etc.

Possible disapproval or perceived disapproval by others on choice of partner

Is a kind supportive partner

Willing to reach out and offer help

A good friend

FOURTH TOE
BROAD TOP JOINT

RIGHT

LEFT

Disposing of surplus objects / possessions difficult but not impossible

Likes to keep friends with everyone

Always admired for knowing the right thing to say at the right time

Sees no reason why they can't maintain a platonic relation ship with former lovers, how could friendship upset anyone

A responsible worker usually the one to stay behind to get things finished

Long lasting loving relationships usually apply, anything less would be most unusual

Tends to keep paperwork in piles but knows where everything is

Tends to be the family leader

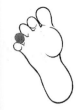

FOURTH TOE
NARROW BASE

RIGHT

LEFT

Restricted from sharing ideas
in early life

Possibly unable to express
emotions in the past

Probably had some difficulty in
standing up for self

A loving person who is wary
of showing true feelings

Female. Perceived Mother/
Mother figure, sister or friend
to display jealous tendencies
towards them

Male. Perceived Father/
Father figure, brother or friend
to display jealous tendencies
towards them

You only see half the capabilities of
this person

Sometimes frustrated by the
actions of others

Afraid of being ridiculed

A loyal friend

FOURTH TOE
LONG

RIGHT

LEFT

Good communication skills

Love and creativity have close links

Confident, especially on issues of relationships

Usually expresses love openly

Caring personality

Compassionate

Good team leader

Might be perceived as a flirt

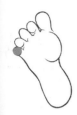

Little Toe
Base hiding under or tucked into toe four

RIGHT	LEFT
May feel insecure	Trust depends on love
May be child of perceived unhappy marriage	Will not become sexually involved without love
May have been bullied or feels bullied	Possibly been hurt in a relationship
Possibly criticised when young	May be a young widow(er) / divorced / separated or feel responsible for family member(s)
May have phobia	Usually a kind nature
Will think of others' feelings	

LITTLE TOE
SQUASHED INTO AND UNDER TOE FOUR

RIGHT	LEFT
May be a little inhibited	Difficulty expressing love
Tends to feel insecure	May question people's motives
May have a tendency towards depression	Feels there is a time from the past best left unexpressed
Probably seeks security	May have had a strict upbringing
A thoughtful nature	May have been bullied by a teacher / tutor / older child
	Often doing good deeds

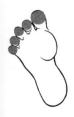 

Big rounded bulbs	-	Good intellect Likes to think things over Good analytical mind, but likes time to prove it
Flattened bulbs (no roundness)	-	May sometimes feel demotivated Feels that life/job is monotonous May feel some ideas fall flat Nice nature
Narrow bulbs	-	Mental rather than physical strengths Logical mind Learns quickly Direct in approach May appear self opinionated during a first encounter but this is generally not the case
Pointed bulbs	-	Good mind Straight to the point In some cases may speak first and think later Would never intentionally hurt, but needs to guard against it happening

Shrivelled bulbs   -   Can have periods of being
                                      withdrawn
                                      May suffer with bouts of
                                      depression or mood swings
                                      Possible past insecurities
                                      Deep thinker

Small dainty bulbs   -   Gentle thoughts / ideas
                                      Not usually forceful in putting
                                      ideas forward
                                      Might suffer from mood swings

Square bulbs   -   Traditionalist
                                      Takes time to accept change (if
                                      at all)
                                      May have a tendency to be critical
                                      Confined thoughts and ideas
                                      Loyal friend

Toe Positions

Bent (Clawing slightly but not enough to be touching the ground)-

Usually lots of stress
May be self-conscious
May feel shame due to the actions of others
Possibly bending to others' ideas
A fear of failure
A fear of taking on responsibility, but will if required
Usually doing kind deeds

Clawing (All toes bent downwards with the tips touching the ground) -

Keeps everything close to the chest
Does not like answering questions about self
Trying to keep in contact with reality
May have struggled to gain credit for abilities
Fear of loss
Perceived domination especially in childhood, this may be due to own sensitivity

TOE POSITIONS CONT.

Button toe   (a tiny button shape obvious on the under bulb of the big toe, when the toes are in contact with the ground) -

> Hidden energy
> Hidden talent
> Would never divulge inner secrets
> All is not what it first may seem
> A head crammed with ideas

Cramped together   -   Grasping ideas
> Not always trusting own ideas
> May feel subdued into conforming, possibly in school, workplace or forces
> Kind nature

Crooked   -   May change thinking to please others
> Might feel unjustly treated by society / superior
> May feel insecure sometimes
> A real friend

Hammer   -   Does not like to bare soul
> Might show aggressive tendencies that help cover true feelings and frustrations
> Could have workaholic tendencies

Raised Tip (tips not in contact with the ground 'slightly raised up') -

Tendency to daydream
Very good imagination
Artistic abilities
Does not like to be confined

Upturned   -   Likes to escape from reality
(toe well raised/   Fantasises
sticking up)   May have a tendency to be
                             argumentative
                             May from time to time behave out of
                             character

Webbed   -   Energy ebbs and flows but never
                             completely lacking
                             May look to others for security

Wide Gaps between -   Deep thinker
                             Assesses worthiness of enquirer
                             before answering questions
                             Knows a lot more than is prepared to
                             share
                             Likes to know all the up-to-date news
                             and gossip but needs time to decipher it

TOE MARKINGS

TOE MARKINGS
TOP

White spots (almost hidden under skin)	-	Unresolved issues Possibly misjudged / unfairly treated

Dimple/indentation like impressions-   Ideas and decisions may be influenced by others
Intellectual thoughts and self opinions may be in conflict

VERTICAL LINES ALONG TOP OF TOES

Centre   -   Thoughts split down the middle
Can see two sides of the argument or two points of view

Down side of toe   -   Wearing a brave face but may have divided feelings
May hide behind a mask

HORIZONTAL LINES

Little toe only   -   May be insecure in home life or work

Across remaining four toes   -   May have been affected by a change in lifestyle or ideas

TOE COLOURS

Blue   -   Injured / bruised ego

Red   -   May feel anger, frustration
                                             Might have dented beliefs
                                             May feel threatened

White   -   Little or no energy
                                             May feel exhausted especially of
                                             mental energy

Yellow / hue   -   Outlook on life may change from
                                             positive to negative
                                             May feel resentful

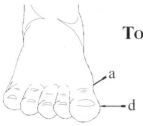

TOE TOPS (DORSUM)
HARD SKIN

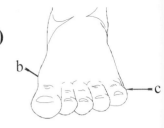

(a) On the joint — Some good ideas may have been quashed or may worry about expressing new ideas

(b) Below the joint — Protection for own thoughts and a guard against possible tendency to be impulsive

(c) On the outside of little toe- Protection from hearing or recognising emotionally disturbing elements of life

(d) On the outside of big toe - Protection - not fully confident with own ideas / inventions / creations

In general, those displaying corns may suffer with stress

Rounded shape tip   -   Thinks before speaking
                                      Good listener
                                      Good negotiator
                                      Tactile person
                                      May lack self confidence
                                      involving own opinions
                                      Considerate of the feelings of
                                      others

Pointed shape   -   May suffer with tension
                                      May give unexpected answers
                                      May suffer with mood swings
                                      I say it as I see it

Obviously blunt   -   Expressive
                                      It is how it is
                                      Copes well outwardly - affected
                                      inwardly
                                      May have a tendency towards
                                      impatience and aggression

Irregular updown shape   -   Uneasy
                                      Worrier
                                      Usually trying to juggle life, love
                                      and emotions

NAILS

Hang nails	-	Seeks support
Ingrowing nails	-	Feels threatened Feels vulnerable
Broken nails	-	May want a change of lifestyle May see self as the family pillar
Thickened nail	-	Perceives a need for extra protection
Spoon shaped nail	-	Lost strength Feels a need to always defend decisions
Weak tearing nails	-	Feeling exposed Vulnerable May display some signs of allergies
Bitten / picked nails	-	Outward weakness covers inner strength Some people suffer break downs- I bite my nails instead

THE USE OF REFLEX POINTS

WHY REFLEX POINTS?

In the following pages I have used some Reflexology Reflex points purely for ease of location for specific areas. It is not intended in any way to link or connect Reflexology and Foot reading.

See chart on pages 144-147

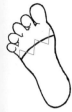
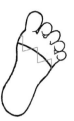

Diaphragm Reflex

Zigzag lines (crisscrossing through the diaphragm line)-

> May be prone to headaches
> May suffer migraines
> Possibly wears glasses/contact lenses
> A deep thinker
> A deep worrier although may keep
> this hidden

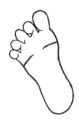
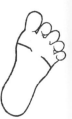

Deep Broken line   -   May have experienced shock
                                     Bereavement
                                     Will probably talk a lot, yet reveal
                                     little
                                     Probably lives/lived an unusual
                                     lifestyle
                                     Life may not be as good or bad as
                                     it first appears
                                     May hide deep sadness

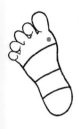

THYROID REFLEX

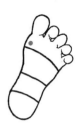

Sunken - Feeling vulnerable
Under attack
Difficult at times to get up and go

Swollen - Possibly unresolved feelings and / or
congested emotions
May lead a demanding life
Little or no time for self

Red - Possible deep-seated anger
May be frustrated due to
commitments to others
Little time to lead own life in the
manner he/she would wish

Hard Skin - Protects personal thoughts
Shields against perceived criticism

Flaking Skin - Changes taking place or wished for
Perfectionist tendencies
Does not like to delegate, why should
they ? The task would probably not be
completed properly.

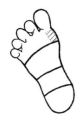 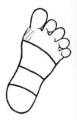

OESOPHAGUS REFLEX

Hard Skin   -   Finds some things in life are
difficult to swallow
Family / friends may not be living up to
expectations
Possibly little or no time for self
Usually unfair demands on time
Possible guilty feelings
May have experienced a shock

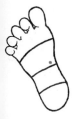
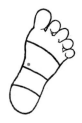

ADRENAL GLAND REFLEX

Swollen   -   Anxiety
A perceived need to be continually
on guard
May occasionally display mood
swings
May need to give more careful
thought to diet and lifestyle

Sunken   -   Lacks energy
May suffer depressive bouts
Possibly felt unable to clearly express
feelings during childhood / teenage
years

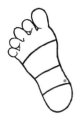 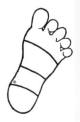

BLADDER REFLEX

Sunken   -   May be trying to make space for progress
May feel life has not always been kind
May be a little depressed at times

Swollen   -   Tension and anxiety restrict the flow
Not sure what to absorb and what to dismiss
May feel that security has been threatened in the past

Red   -   Can feel anxious, overworked
Guilt or embarrassment related to a family member or friend
May feel some anger towards a partner or very close friend

Hard Skin   -   May feel stuck in a rut
Sometimes feels it can be difficult to move forward, but will always be looking for ways to acheive aims

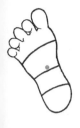 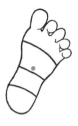

KIDNEY REFLEX

Sunken   -   May feel drained mentally and
physically
Inner struggle to deal with the burden
of life

Swollen   -   Difficulty dealing with additional stress
Trying to sort out what's right from
what's wrong
A go-between
Usually able to resolve problems for
others

Red   -   May feel fed up with the perceived lack
of structure in the work place or home
situation
May feel others are not doing
their share

Hard Skin   -   Protection of physical and/or emotional
self

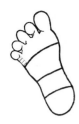

SHOULDER REFLEX

Sunken   -   May be giving in to pressures
Possible uncertainty regarding
self-worth
May doubt own capabilities

Swollen   -   Sometimes feels weighed down
May feel pressures of life/work/home
have been or are becoming
overwhelming
May have emotional conflict

Hard Skin   -   Protection from being burdened by
the problems of others
Has to push a way through their life
Sometimes it seems nothing in life
comes easy

Broad   -   Trying to find space for own life
and emotions
May be longing for freedom and
change
May be resisting any further
responsibility

 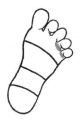

EAR REFLEX

Hard skin   -   I have heard too many problems
I don't want to hear what I can't
deal with
I don't want any ear problems

Swollen   -   I am struggling to hear
I am struggling to learn
Subjected to real or perceived noise
Why should I have ear problems, I have
too much to do and no time to do it

Red   -   May have a wax build up
Some of what I have to listen to makes
me angry inside
There may be bullying in the home or
workplace

Sunken   -   I think my hearing is not as good as it
could be
I have had a knock on that ear
I used to have ear problems
I sometimes have ear problems

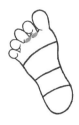

Eye reflex

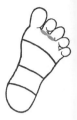

Sunken	-	Low energy I am tired of reading or seeing the same old thing Sometimes I cannot make sense of my life
Swollen	-	Overworked Eyestrain May need to change eye glasses / contact lenses
Red	-	Some of what I have to look at makes me angry There could be an unfair situation developing in the workplace or home
Hard Skin	-	Protection Helps me deal with the things I see and cannot change

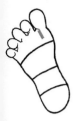
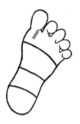

TRACHEA REFLEX

Hard skin   -   Feeling choked
Cannot always express true feelings
May worry about lots of things
Perceived pressure from superiors/
guardians / parents

Deep lines / crevice -   Has possibly suffered a shock in the
past
May sometimes suffer fear /
uncertainty
May lack confidence in expressing
own abilities
May sometimes feel breathless /
speechless

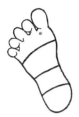

Hard skin   -   Protection
May have endured unpleasant
comments
Perceived deformity of skeleton

Sunken   -   Physical work too heavy
Needs more sunshine in life
May sometimes speak before
thinking

Swollen   -   May feel heavily laden due to thoughts
or action of others
Life is sometimes a bit of a burden
May have some pent up emotions

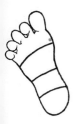

THYMUS REFLEX

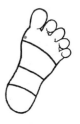

Hard skin   -   Protection
                                  Trying to hide vulnerability
                                  Keeping others at bay
                                  I don't want to catch something

Sunken   -   Lowered self-esteem
                                  Feeling vulnerable
                                  Lacking strength / lessened resistance
                                  It's a fight to keep going
                                  Immune system needs a boost

Swollen   -   To much demand on energy
                                  No personal space
                                  I am surrounded by sick people
                                  I must keep going at any cost

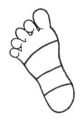

HEART REFLEX
LEFT FOOT ONLY

Hard skin   -   Protective shield
Possible guard against emotional hurt
Helps me to cope with observations of
suffering endured by others
The feet of a carer

Lines   Deep -   Broken heart / emotional
Bereavement

           Slight -   Emotional changes
Changes in life and circumstances
Philosophical

Red   -   Deep emotional hurt
Pent up anger
It was not my fault so why did it happen

SMALL INTESTINE REFLEX

Swollen   -   May feel trapped in a relationship
                                     May feel trapped at work
                                     May experience some difficulty in
                                     communicating feelings
                                     Own expectations may be too high

Red bulge   -   Lacking energy in digestive system
(see white dot on diagram)

NOTE! Bulge may appear / disappear according to energy levels

Large Intestine / Colon Reflex

Swollen   -   May close mind to new ideas limiting
                          expansion
                          Burdened with the problems of others
                          May be afraid to let go physically and
                          emotionally
                          May be feeling bitter or angry about
                          something in the past

Sunken   -   Has dealt with a deep hurt of the past
                          Low energy levels
                          May suffer from inferiority complex
                          May be hesitant to voice own
                          opinions

SPINE REFLEX

7 CERVICAL VERTEBRAE SLIGHTLY
RIGID / PAINFUL

-     May be seeking new ideas in order to move forward
  Tension and stress
  Holding the head and neck rigid to spite what life has dished up in the past
  Seeking help to support their thoughts and wishes
  May be feeling insecure

SPINE REFLEX

12 THORACIC VERTEBRAE SLIGHTLY RIGID / PAINFUL

- May feel as if their back is against the wall
  Shouldering a lot of responsibility
  Holding a secret close to the chest
  Always does more than duty requires
  May be a little stubborn
  Strongly principled
  May carry a heavy emotional burden

SPINE REFLEX

5 LUMBAR VERTEBRAE SLIGHTLY
STIFF / PAINFUL

- May have taken the blame for the wrongful actions of others
  Possibly spends life in the service of others
  Perceived obstacles to progress
  May seek solidarity
  Feels others may take advantage of them

SPINE REFLEX

5 SACRUM STIFF / PAINFUL

- Possible resentment at the perceived injustices of life
  May have some guilt regarding relationships
  Perceived lack of emotional support
  Reliable and flexible with friends
  May be worried about own capabilities
  May have supported self from an early age or had very strong opinions about own future

4 COCCYX STIFF / PAINFUL

- May have problems handling the details of life
  Expectations may be out of reach
  May feel as though losing grip on situations or problems that need to be acted upon
  May be resentful at the feeling of being under someone else's control
  May be concerned about own gender
  May try too hard to help others at the expense of own health/quality time

SOLAR PLEXUS REFLEX

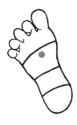

SOLAR PLEXUS REFLEX

Sunken   -   Perceives past life as not always
having been kind
Little time for self due to the
demands of others
Probably felt grown-up at a very
early age
Possible guilt about someone from the
past

Swollen   -   A struggle to maintain the
perceived self image created
by others
May have survived an occupation or
home situation against a lot of odds
Is most likely stressed and worried

Red   -   Fed up with the lack of structure in
the work place or home situation
Having to cope with others not doing
their share
Would like more quality time

Hard Skin   -   True thoughts and feelings concealed
Protection
Has developed a way to shield self
against that which is unexpected

SOLAR PLEXUS REFLEX
LINES

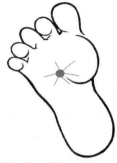

Coming from

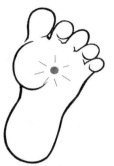

Going towards

Lines defined as leaving the solar plexus are those lines in contact with the area and radiating outwards away from the solar plexus.

Lines defined as going towards the solar plexus are those lines radiating towards and stopping just short of the solar plexus.

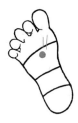 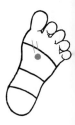

LINES LEADING TOWARDS THE
SOLAR PLEXUS REFLEX

From the big toe

Right Foot   -   Overworked mind and little time to deal with emotional thoughts, the future or perceived upsets
A setback, possibly did not progress through school or through a training programme as originally planned or desired
Trying to establish own independent business or perhaps position of seniority or may be in a new work environment

Left Foot   -   A broken relationship partly due to lack of time given to allow for growth and development
Possible work or business taking priority
A bereavement may have influenced change in lifestyle
May have experienced a deep sadness

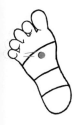
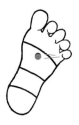

LINES LEADING TOWARDS THE
SOLAR PLEXUS REFLEX

From the little toe

Right Foot — May have experienced insecurity in childhood
Possible separation from parent (one or both)
May have been bullied
Sought and may still seek materialistic security and sees material possessions as security

Left Foot — Possibly lacks confidence in own abilities to attract those of the opposite sex though no need to feel this way
May be insecure in relationship
Possibly shy in expressing feelings in a close relationship
May rush into relationships that end with some problems

Towards the little toe

Either Foot   -   May be parted from loved ones
                                Possibly experienced bereavement of a
                                close friend or younger family member
                                May be searching for security
                                May have been looked after by nanny or
                                similar in formative years
                                A fear of loss

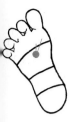

LINES LEAVING THE
SOLAR PLEXUS REFLEX

Towards the big toe

Either Foot   -   A changed lifestyle
                                May need to examine diet
                                A possible relationship breakdown
                                May feel material possessions are
                                necessary for emotional stability
                                May often be misread in first
                                impressions
                                Kind hearted but not always repaid

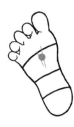
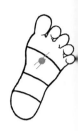

VERTICAL LINES THROUGH THE CENTRE OF
THE SOLAR PLEXUS REFLEX

One or more lines through the centre of the Solar Plexus reflex usually suggest heartache. If deeper on the left foot, this usually suggests a bereavement.

Lines from the Solar Plexus longer upwards towards the toes rather than downwards into foot may suggest a hurt or bereavement that is still very fresh in the mind or that there is a lasting scar.

Lines longer downwards into the foot rather than upwards towards the toes may suggest a hurt or bereavement of longer duration, or a hurt or bereavement that has been rationalised and dealt with.

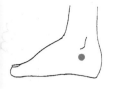

Uterus (female) or
Prostate (male) Reflex

Sunken   -   Lacking in energy
                              Perceived prejudices against female
                              or male gender
                              Possible past emotional abuse

Swollen   -   May lack security
                              Possible unresolved issues related to
                              gender
                              Possible frustration towards a partner
                              May be reluctant to let go of the past
                              Female may be pregnant

Red   -   Possible frustration with life
                              May be going through emotional
                              turmoil
                              May have fallen in love when very
                              young

Deep line underneath -   May feel pulled emotionally in two
                              directions
                              Unfulfilled promise to self
                              Possibly a broken promise by someone
                              else

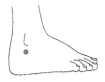

OVARY (FEMALE) OR
TESTICLE (MALE) REFLEX

Swollen   -   Inner crying
                                      Emotional burden
                                      Losing a grip on a relationship
                                      Losing confidence in own abilities
                                      Lacking energy
                                      Lacking confidence in own gender /
                                      abilities

Red   -   Perceived lack of emotional support

Lung Reflex

Sunken — Loathes confrontation
May have suffered a disappointment
in a love or family relationship
May have withdrawn from an
active life or be giving too much of
self to others

Swollen — Perhaps there is a family conflict
May have a tendency towards
obstinacy
May be suffering emotional or
physical congestion

Hard Skin — Provides a shield
Protects own space
Spends life taking care of others
A deep emotional shock in life

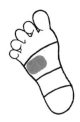

LIVER REFLEX
RIGHT FOOT ONLY

Sunken   -   Suppressed emotions
Frustrated at lack of time for self
Stored anger due to perceived
injustices in the past

Swollen   -   May lack energy
Perceives that a partner, friend or
family member is unfaithful, disloyal
and not to be trusted
May be having to cope with a heavy
load that is becoming increasingly
difficult to cope with

Pancreas Reflex

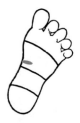

Sunken   -   A bitter pill might have been difficult to swallow, either in the past or currently
Possibly dealing with a change in life-style or occupation, not necessarily enjoyable

Swollen   -   Possibly suffers a lack of enthusiasm for a new idea
May not always feel in control of own destiny
May feel overloaded with having to deal with the physical and emotional problems of others

Note!   The left foot reflex will be more obvious than the right foot.

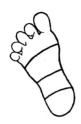

RECTUM / ANUS REFLEX
LEFT FOOT ONLY

Sunken   -   Low energy
Life, love and work unbalanced in
favour of others
May feel they have paid a high price
for freedom

Swollen   -   Squirrel like hoarding
May be resenting change
Afraid of loss, either emotional or
material

Tender   -   Holds in emotions
May feel dominated or bullied
Possibly lacks the confidence to stand
up for self

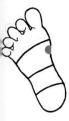

Stomach Reflex

Sunken - Allergies
Hurt to the pit of my stomach
May have suffered much emotionally
Perhaps memory is not quite what it
used to be
May have food eating fads

Swollen - May suffer anguish
A favourite food, not necessarily the
most nutritious
May feel there is no choice but to
continue a less than ideal lifestyle
May feel a little weighed down with
problems and worry

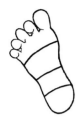

SPLEEN REFLEX
LEFT FOOT ONLY

Sunken   -   Let each lead his/her life as he/she
                           sees fit
                           Low energy
                           Little time to rest

Swollen   -   A sensitive nature
                           May have obsessive tendencies
                           Will usually find the right words
                           when faced with a most difficult
                           situation

Footcharts
These charts may be used as a guide to area location

Right Foot

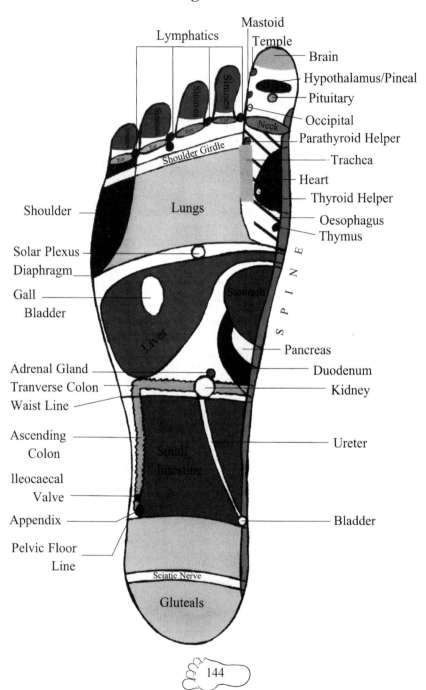

Lymphatics

Mastoid
Temple
Brain
Hypothalamus/Pineal
Pituitary
Occipital
Parathyroid Helper
Trachea
Heart
Thyroid Helper
Oesophagus
Thymus

Sinuses
Neck
Shoulder Girdle
Ear

Shoulder

Lungs

SPINE

Solar Plexus
Diaphragm

Gall
Bladder

Stomach

Liver

Pancreas

Adrenal Gland
Tranverse Colon
Waist Line

Duodenum
Kidney

Ascending
Colon

Small
Intestine

Ureter

lleocaecal
Valve

Appendix

Bladder

Pelvic Floor
Line

Sciatic Nerve

Gluteals

Left Foot

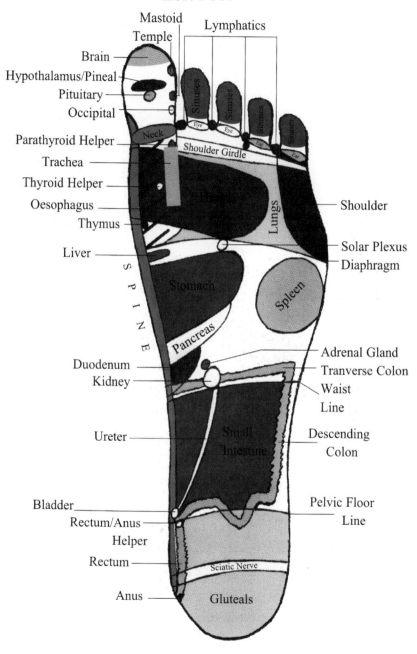

Mastoid
Temple
Brain
Hypothalamus/Pineal
Pituitary
Occipital
Parathyroid Helper
Trachea
Thyroid Helper
Oesophagus
Thymus
Liver
Duodenum
Kidney
Ureter
Bladder
Rectum/Anus Helper
Rectum
Anus

Lymphatics
Sinuses
Sinuses
Sinuses
Sinuses
Eye
Eye
Ear
Ear
Neck
Shoulder Girdle
Lungs
Shoulder
Solar Plexus
Diaphragm
SPINE
Stomach
Spleen
Pancreas
Adrenal Gland
Tranverse Colon
Waist Line
Small Intestine
Descending Colon
Pelvic Floor Line
Sciatic Nerve
Gluteals

145

Right Foot

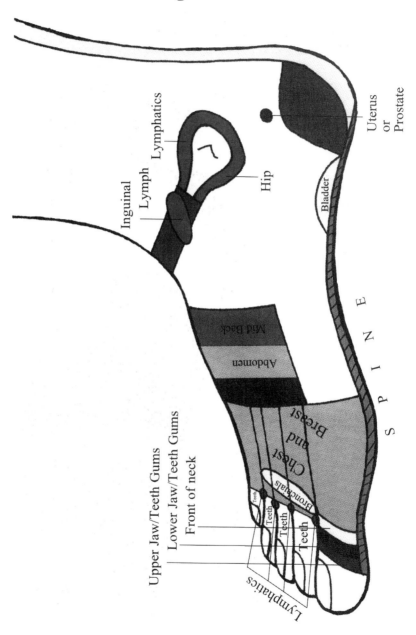

Left Foot

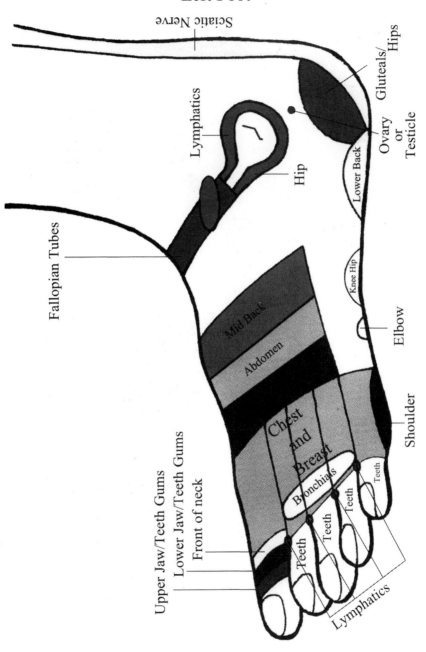

Sciatic Nerve

Gluteals/Hips

Lymphatics

Ovary or Testicle

Hip

Lower Back

Fallopian Tubes

Knee Hip

Elbow

Mid Back

Abdomen

Chest and Breast

Shoulder

Bronchias

Teeth

Upper Jaw/Teeth Gums
Lower Jaw/Teeth Gums
Front of neck

Teeth

Lymphatics

ARTIST'S IMPRESSIONS OF SOME TOE TYPES

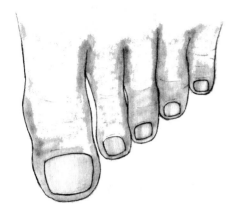

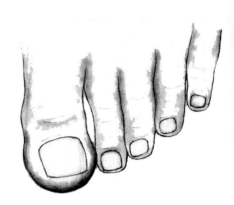

Fourth toe broad top joint   **Big toe broad at base**

Broad big toe

 148

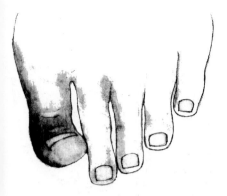

Upturned toe

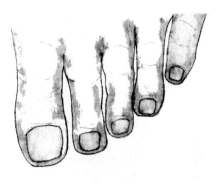

Toe 2 out of proportion

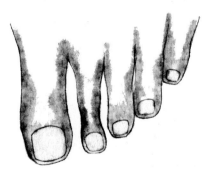

Toe 2 very thin

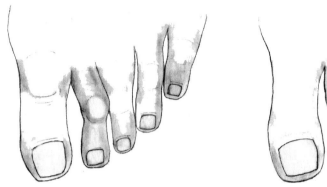

Crooked toe 2   **Toe 2 tilting towards toe 3**

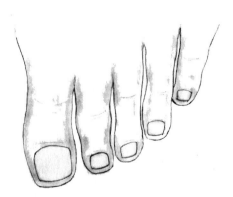

Toe 2 broad top joint

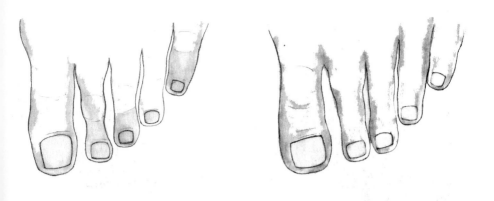

Toe 2 narrow top joint

Toe 3 equal to toe 2

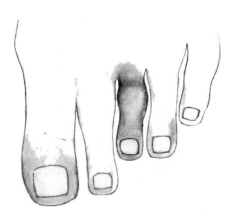

Hammer toe 3, raised middle joint

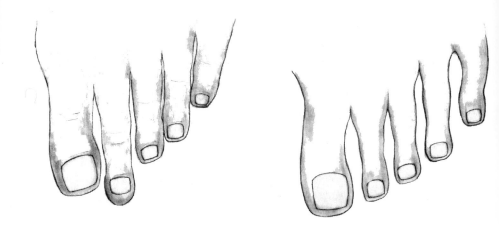

Toe 2 longer than toe 1　　　　　　**Wide gap, open toed**

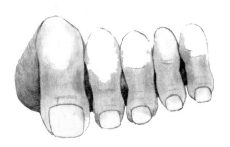

Clawing, all toes bent down

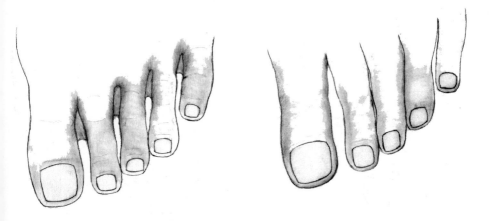

Webbed toes   **Broad top joint fourth toe**

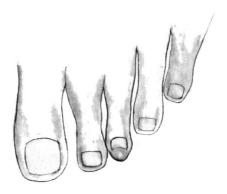

**When toe on floor bulb is
visible underneath**

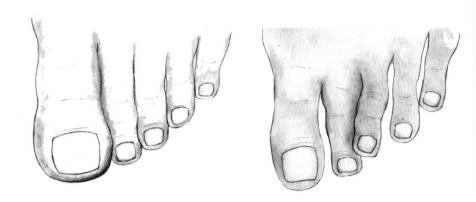

Cramped together toes **Toe 3 over toe 2**

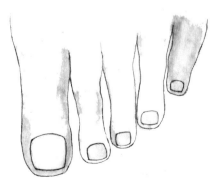

**Third toe narrow middle
joint**

INDEX

Index

P

R

S

W

Y

Qualified Reflexologists

Foot Reading for the Therapist

is

Information pertinent to the practitioner.

This text will encourage deeper visual attention which in turn will aid your practical skill and understanding of Reflexology.

The information is based on almost forty years experience and examination of more than thirty thousand pairs of feet, there is nothing comparable in print.

To obtain your copy simply complete the application form on the reverse and send it together with your remittance, **copies** of relevant qualifications and/or relevant membership certificates should also be enclosed.

ORDERING YOUR COPY OF
FOOT READING FOR THE THERAPIST

FOR JUST £14.99

PLUS POSATGE AND PAKING
UK, EIRE, CHANNEL ISLANDS AND EUROPE £3.00
OTHER £5.00

It is possible to order this exciting additon in two ways,

• By Creditcard over the telepone
on 020 8680 9631

• By sending a cheque/Postal order/Sterling Bank Draft to

D.B.P. First Floor Suite, 253 Selhurst Road, London, SE25 6XT